Atlantic Adventure

Michael Perham and Alex Lane ■ Jonatronix

Contents

OXFORD
UNIVERSITY PRESS

Record breaking!

On 3rd January 2007, Michael Perham broke a world record!
He became the youngest person to sail across the Atlantic Ocean by himself.
He was only 14 years old.
It took him just over 6 weeks. He sailed more than 4700 miles.

What a long way.

North Atlantic Ocean

Start

Finish

Wow! That's so brave!

South Atlantic Ocean

Michael on his boat.

Learning to sail

Michael started sailing when he was 6 years old. He was taught to sail by his dad. Michael started by sailing small boats.

Michael and his dad, Peter.

It's harder than it looks!

Michael learning to row. His mum is watching.

In 2003, a 15-year-old boy sailed across the Atlantic Ocean all by himself. It was a new world record. Michael wanted to beat this record.

Michael started to train for *his* Atlantic trip. He trained for over a year and sailed many miles.

Michael's fact box

When was Michael born?	16th March, 1992
Where does he live?	Hertfordshire, England
What are his interests?	• Anything to do with water and sailing • music • playing the drums • skiing • bike jumping.

Cheeky Monkey

Michael needed a good boat for his long journey. The type of boat he used was a *Tide 28*.
Michael helped to design it himself.
He called his boat *Cheeky Monkey*.

Cheeky Monkey was a small, fast boat. It was made from light, strong materials so that it floated easily on top of the waves.

mast

sails

motor

safety rail

Michael's route

Michael started his Atlantic trip in Gibraltar. First he sailed down the coast of Africa. Then he sailed out to open water. He had two stops on the way. Michael's dad sailed near him in another boat in case he got into trouble.

Can you imagine travelling that far?

USA

ATLANTIC OCEAN

Finish: Antigua

CARIBBEAN

Michael finished in Antigua. The journey was more than 4700 nautical miles.
A nautical mile is a mile at sea. It is a bit longer than a mile on land.

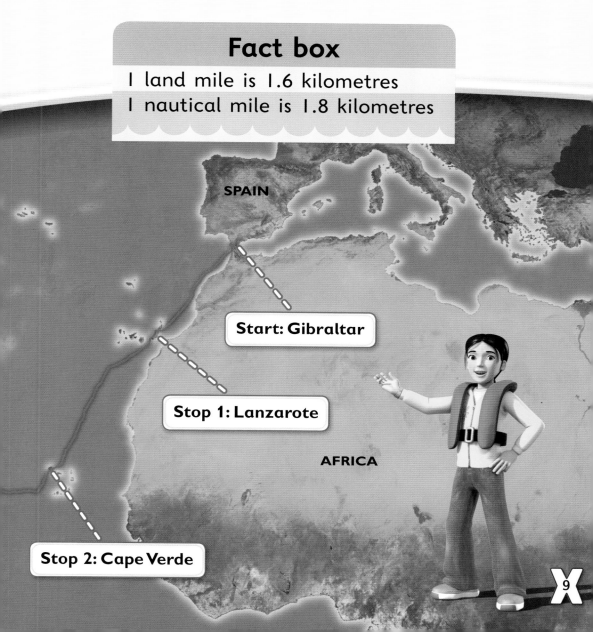

Fact box

1 land mile is 1.6 kilometres
1 nautical mile is 1.8 kilometres

SPAIN

Start: Gibraltar

Stop 1: Lanzarote

AFRICA

Stop 2: Cape Verde

Packing up

There is no fresh water at sea. Michael had to make sure that he had enough for the whole trip.

What food would you miss most?

Michael also took a lot of tinned food. The food he missed most was warm toast and pizza.

It could get very cold at night. Michael had to make sure that he had warm clothes with him. Sometimes the waves would splash Michael. It was hard to keep dry!

Setting out

After a year of getting ready, Michael finally set sail.
During his trip Michael kept a **blog**.
This meant that other people could read about his adventure on the Internet.

Have you ever kept a diary or a blog?

Michael and his dad doing some last minute checks before setting off!

Extract from Michael's blog: 18th November, 2006

We left at 1pm. We were going to leave a bit earlier but we waited for the wind to pick up. We are so excited. My dad is so proud of me!

A view of the Atlantic from the back of *Cheeky Monkey*.

Wind and waves

Sailing boats need wind to get them to go.
Wind fills the sails and pushes the boat along.
When there was no wind, Michael's boat
would drift around and not go far.

Calm winds mean
gentle sailing.

At other times, the wind would be very strong. A sudden gust of wind is called a squall. Strong winds meant there were some big waves. Some were over 7 metres high. Luckily Michael does not get sea sick!

Strong winds mean big waves which are great for surfing!

What to see at sea

You might think that there is nothing to look at at sea. But Michael saw lots of things ...

Extract from Michael's blog: 4th December, 2006

Had a fantastic display of dolphins before sunset. They must have been with the boat for at least 2 hours. They were jumping up in the air and being crazy. One dolphin made a huge jump out of the top of a wave. It was amazing.

dolphin

Michael took this photo of a dolphin from his boat.

Another flying fish jumped into the **cockpit** today. My dad said he saw a great long shark following him when we were drifting around. It was about 4 metres long! Scary stuff. I'm glad that didn't jump into my cockpit!

17

Life on board

Michael and his dad were sailing the same way but they were often quite far apart. Once Michael did not see his dad's boat for three days!

They kept in contact by **satellite** phone and by radio.

The radio inside the cabin of *Cheeky Monkey*.

speaker

radio

map

Can you think of all the different ways that people keep in touch with one another?

Michael had to do lots of jobs on the boat.

JOBS TO DO:
* sailor
* navigator
* cook
* cleaner
* repairman

Resting and relaxing

It is not easy to get a good night's sleep when you are sailing by yourself. Michael could only rest for a little while each time. To relax, Michael listened to music and read books. He also played games over the radio with his dad.

Michael said that he missed his friends.
He got a bit lonely at times.
As he got near the end of his adventure,
Michael began counting down the miles and
the hours. He was looking forward to a good
meal and a solid bed!

What would you miss most if you were away from home for 6 weeks?

The end of the adventure

When Michael finally arrived in Antigua, he was very tired but very happy. He got a great welcome. About 2000 people came out to meet him!

Extract from Michael's blog: 3rd January, 2007

Going into harbour there were at least 50 small boats following us. They were tooting their horns and saying well done. It was amazing. The big boats were also tooting their horns and there were flags flying. It was fantastic.

Now Michael wants to be the first person to sail, drive and fly round the world by himself. Make sure you look out for him in the news.

Michael arrives in Antigua!

Glossary

blog   an on-line diary

cockpit   an area on the boat where it is
                steered from

mast   a tall pole that holds up a
                ship's sails

motor   an engine that makes a
                machine go

sail   a large piece of strong cloth
                which makes a boat move along
                when the wind blows into it

satellite   a spacecraft that moves around
                the Earth and sends signals down
                to it

Index